Hawaii

Activity Book
for Kids

This Activity Book
Belongs To:

_____

_____

Welcome to Hawaii!

Welcome to Hawaii, a beautiful and magical place filled with sun, sand, and lots of fun!. In this activity book, we'll learn some cool facts about Hawaii, the capital city, and the amazing things you can do there.

Hawaii is a beautiful group of islands located in the middle of the Pacific Ocean. It's the only state in the United States that is made up entirely of islands.

The islands are home to stunning active volcanoes, where lava flows and creates new land.

The capital city of Hawaii is Honolulu. It's located on the island of Oahu, which is known for its stunning beaches and vibrant city life.

Hawaii is made up of 137 islands, but only a few of them are big enough for people to live on.
The main islands are Hawaii (also known as the Big Island), Maui, Oahu, Kauai, Molokai, and Lanai.

Let's embark on an exciting journey to discover the wonders of this tropical paradise!

Hawaii is known as the "Aloha State" because of the warm and friendly spirit of its people.

Hula dancing is a traditional Hawaiian dance form that tells stories through graceful movements

The ukulele

The ukulele is a musical instrument that's a lot of fun to play!
It looks like a small guitar with four strings. The word
"ukulele" actually means "jumping flea" in Hawaiian because
when people first saw it, they thought the players' fingers
looked like little jumping fleas! The ukulele originated in
Hawaii and has become popular all around the world

TIKI

Tiki is a special kind of artwork that comes from the Polynesian cultures, like those in Hawaii. It's all about carved statues made from wood. These statues are called Tiki and they have their own unique meanings and importance.

Dive into the vibrant marine ecosystem of Hawaii!

Discover colorful coral reefs

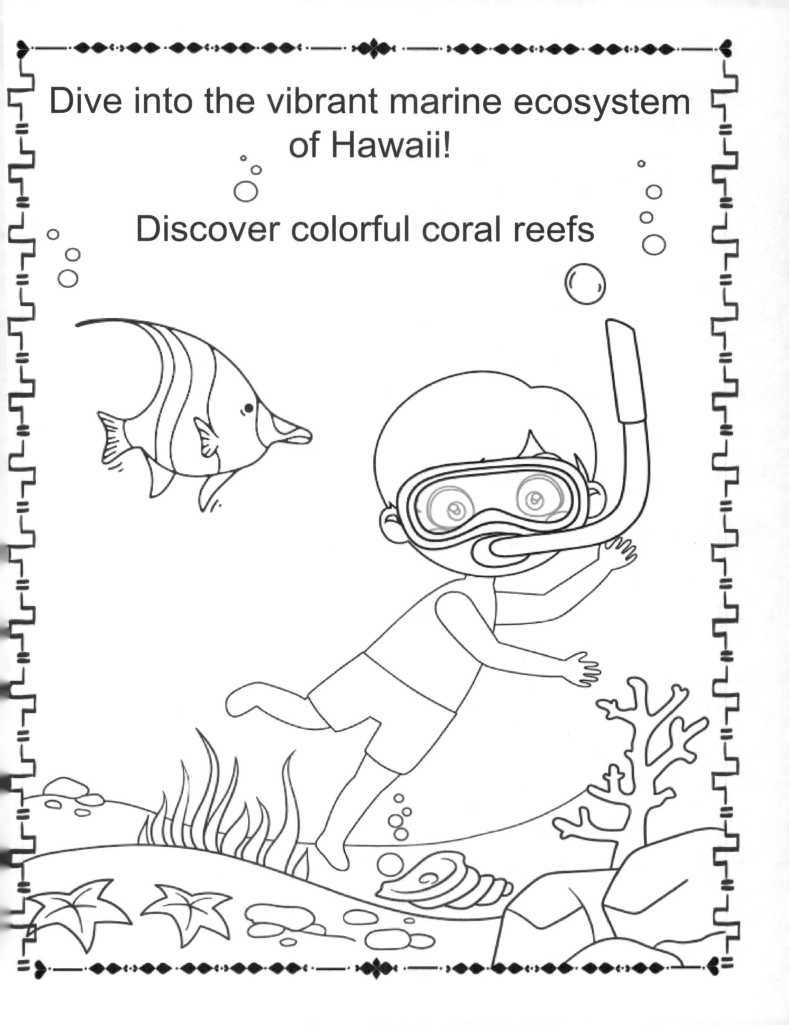

Did you know that coral reefs are like underwater cities full of colorful homes? Coral reefs are made up of tiny animals called coral polyps. These polyps build hard, rocky structures called coral reefs over many years

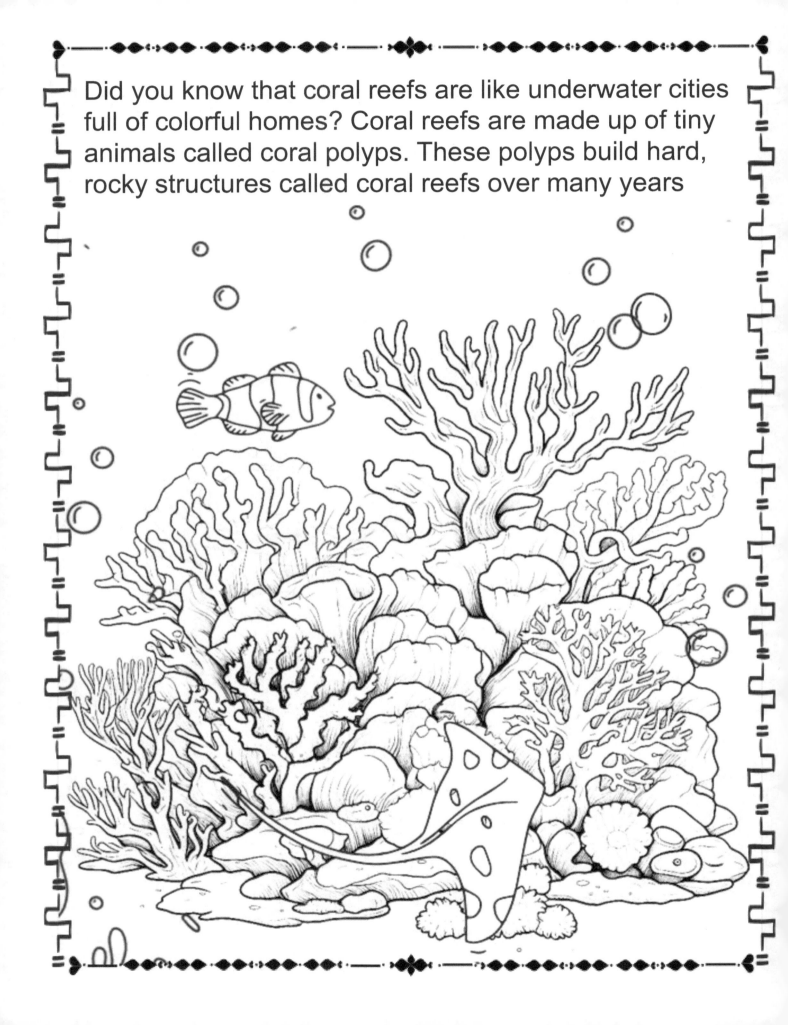

Playful dolphin

Majestic sea turtle

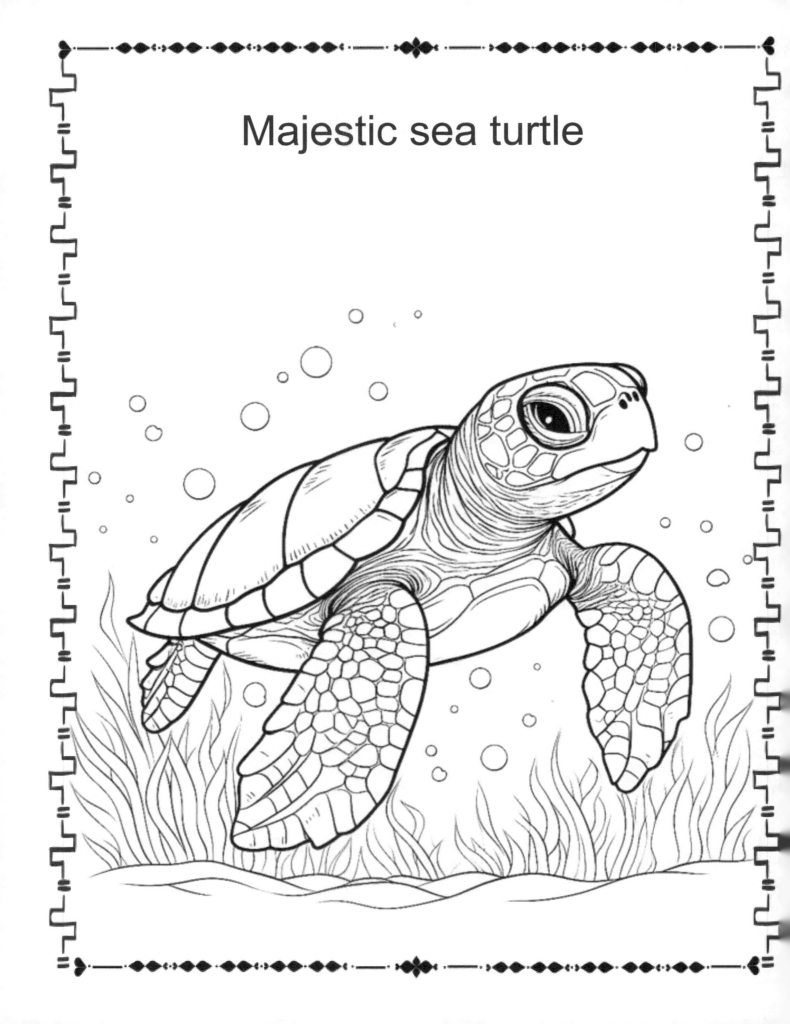

Moorish Idol,

Known for its striking black, white, and yellow patterns, the Moorish Idol is a common sight in Hawaiian waters

Unique Animals of Hawaii
Meet some of Hawaii's unique animals.

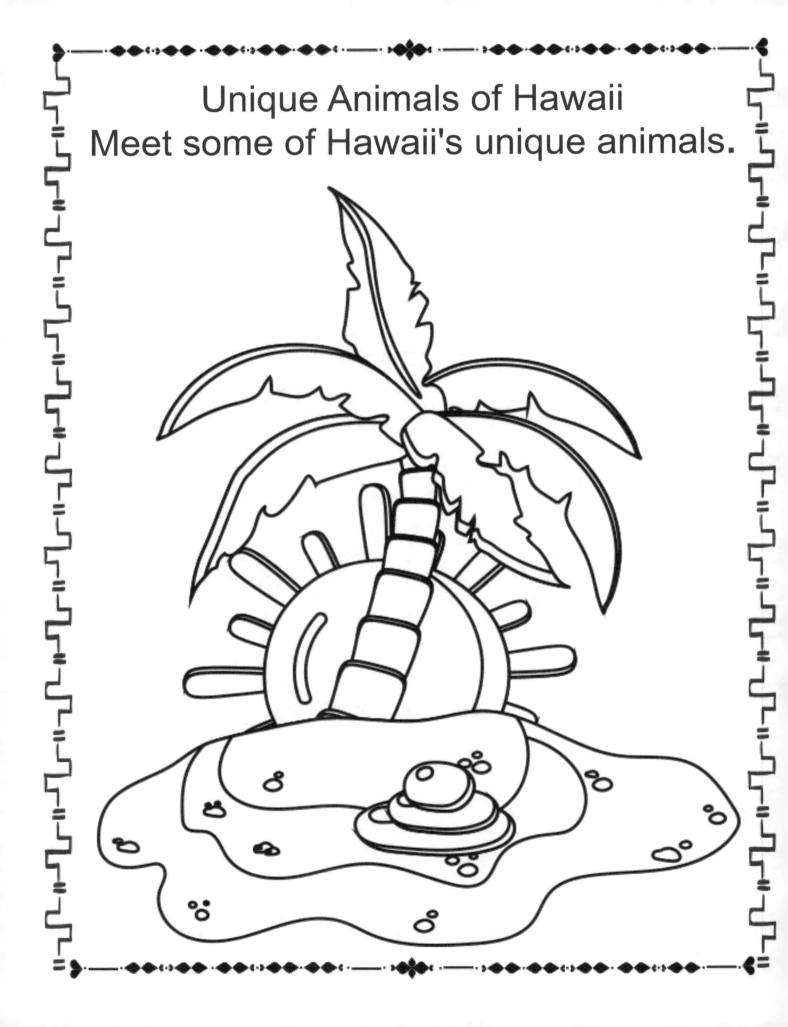

The Hawaiian monk seal,
a friendly marine mammal,
loves to bask in the sun on sandy beaches.

The nene,
a rare goose found only in Hawaii,
is a symbol of the islands' natural beauty.

Surf's Up!
Hang ten and catch some waves in Hawaii!

Learn about the sport of surfing and famous surf spots like Waikiki Beach.

Surfing is a thrilling water sport where you balance on a surfboard and ride the waves. Hawaii is famous for its incredible surf spots, and one of the most iconic places to catch a wave is Waikiki Beach. With its warm waters and gentle waves, Waikiki Beach is a perfect spot for beginners to learn how to surf. Surfers from all around the world gather here to ride the waves and feel the exhilaration of gliding across the water. So grab your surfboard and let's hit the waves at Waikiki Beach!

Can you imagine riding the big waves like a pro?

Hawaiian leis

Hawaiian leis are beautiful garlands made with love and special flowers.
Discover the different flowers used to make these beautiful garlands.
There are many different flowers used to make leis in Hawaii!
One popular flower is the fragrant and colorful plumeria. It has soft petals in shades of white, pink, yellow, and more.

Another flower often used is the vibrant and cheerful hibiscus. Its large, trumpet-shaped blooms come in various colors like red, yellow, and orange. You might also find leis made with pretty orchids, which have delicate petals and come in stunning shades like purple, pink, and white. These flowers, with their lovely scents and vibrant colors, make Hawaiian leis extra special!

Plumeria

Hbiscus

Orchid

Hawaii's state symbols

The nene, the state bird, is a protected species found only in Hawaii.

The yellow hibiscus is the state flower, representing beauty and sunshine.

The kukui tree, the state tree, provides useful nuts and oil.

Aloha shirts are colorful and floral-printed shirts popular in Hawaii.

Hawaiian Traditional Food

Hawaii has a special blend of cultural influences that make its food extra tasty. One popular dish is called poke (pronounced poh-kay). It's like a tasty bowl of cubed raw fish mixed with yummy ingredients like soy sauce, sesame oil, and fresh vegetables. Another Hawaiian favorite is the sweet and tangy pineapple. Did you know that Hawaii is famous for growing some of the juiciest and most delicious pineapples in the world? You can also try poi, a traditional Hawaiian dish made from pounded taro root. It has a unique texture and is often enjoyed with other Hawaiian dishes.

In Hawaii, you can find a variety of delicious and tropical fruits. Here are some famous fruits

Pineapple

Hawaii is famous for its sweet and juicy pineapples. The tropical climate of the islands provides the perfect conditions for growing these flavorful fruits.

Coconut

Coconuts are another iconic fruit in Hawaii.

Mango

Mangoes are a popular fruit in Hawaii, known for their sweet and juicy flavor

Papaya

Papayas are tropical fruits with a vibrant orange flesh. They are packed with vitamins and have a sweet, slightly tangy taste that kids might enjoy.

Passion Fruit

Passion fruit, with its wrinkled purple or yellow skin, is a unique and tangy fruit that can be found in Hawaii.

Mahalo!

Mahalo means "thank you" in Hawaiian.
We hope you enjoyed this glimpse into the
wonders of Hawaii!
Get ready to have fun with puzzles, coloring
pages, and more in this activity book!

Hawaii crossword

COMPLETE THE CROSSWORD PUZZLE BELOW

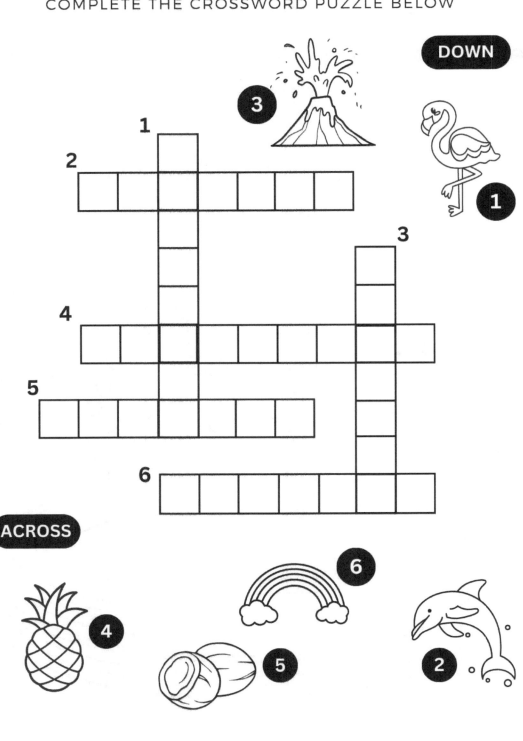

DOWN

ACROSS

Count and color

Hawaii Crossword

COMPLETE THE CROSSWORD PUZZLE BELOW

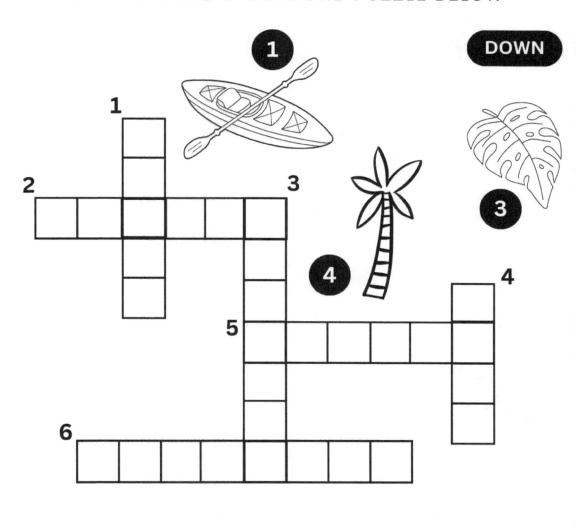

1

DOWN

3

4

ACROSS

2

5

6

Count and color

Maze game

Spot 5 differences

Match word with picture

Lei •   • (coconut)

Coconut •   • (volcano)

Pineapple •   • (palm tree)

Volcano •   • (shirt)

Palm •   • (pineapple)

Shirt •   • (lei)

Maze game

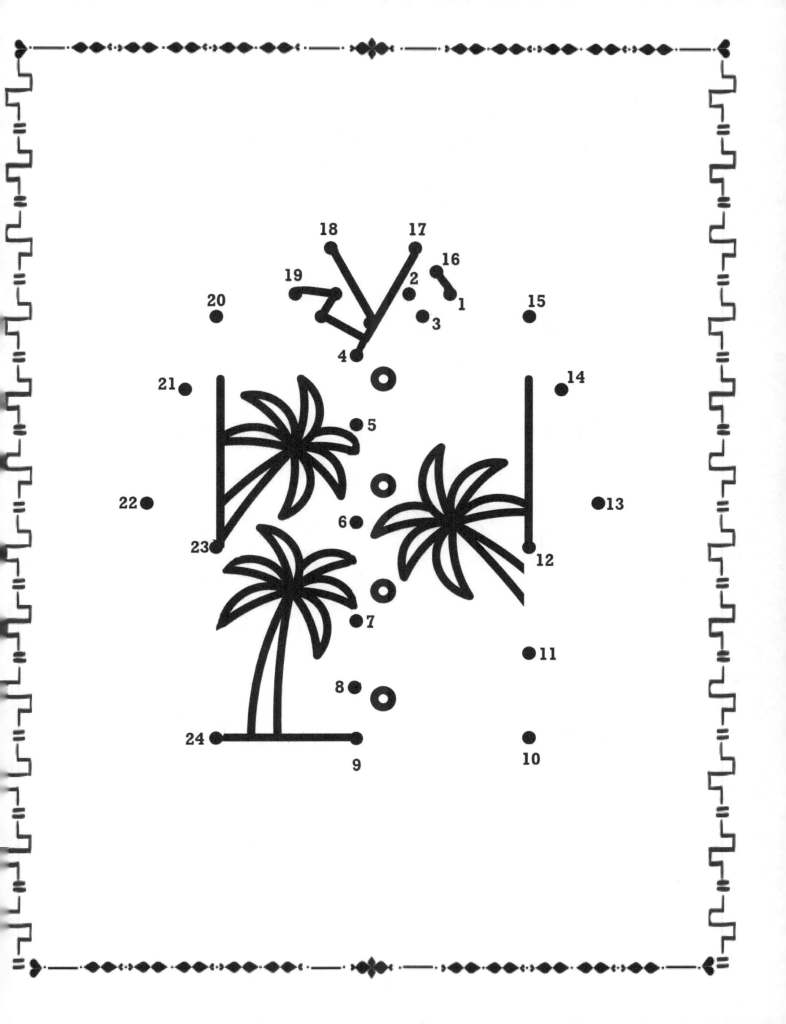

Match word with picture

Dolphin •

Papaya •

Plumeria •

Canoe •

Hibiscus •

Crab •

Hawaii CROSSWORD

Across:

2 A garland or wreath made of flowers, shells, or leaves.

3 A Hawaiian dance that has flowing hand and hip movements.

5 A popular Hawaiian greeting

Down:

1 A tropical fruit with a spiky exterior and sweet flesh

4 A Hawaiian feast.

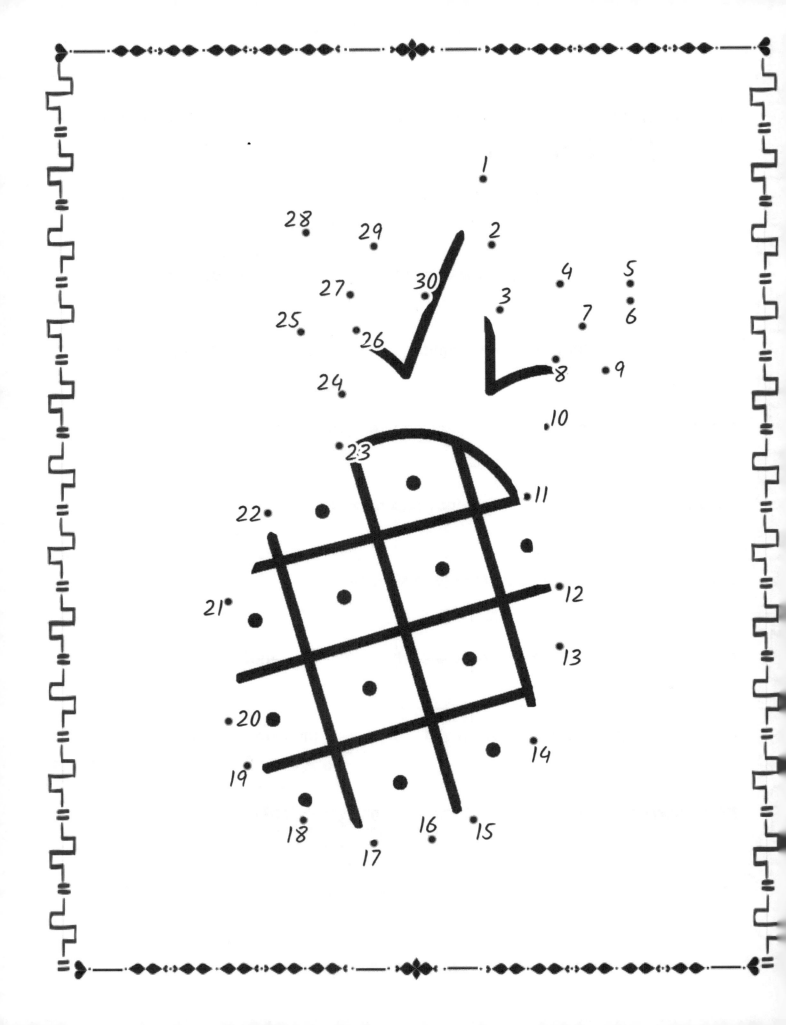

Maze Game

spot 5 differences

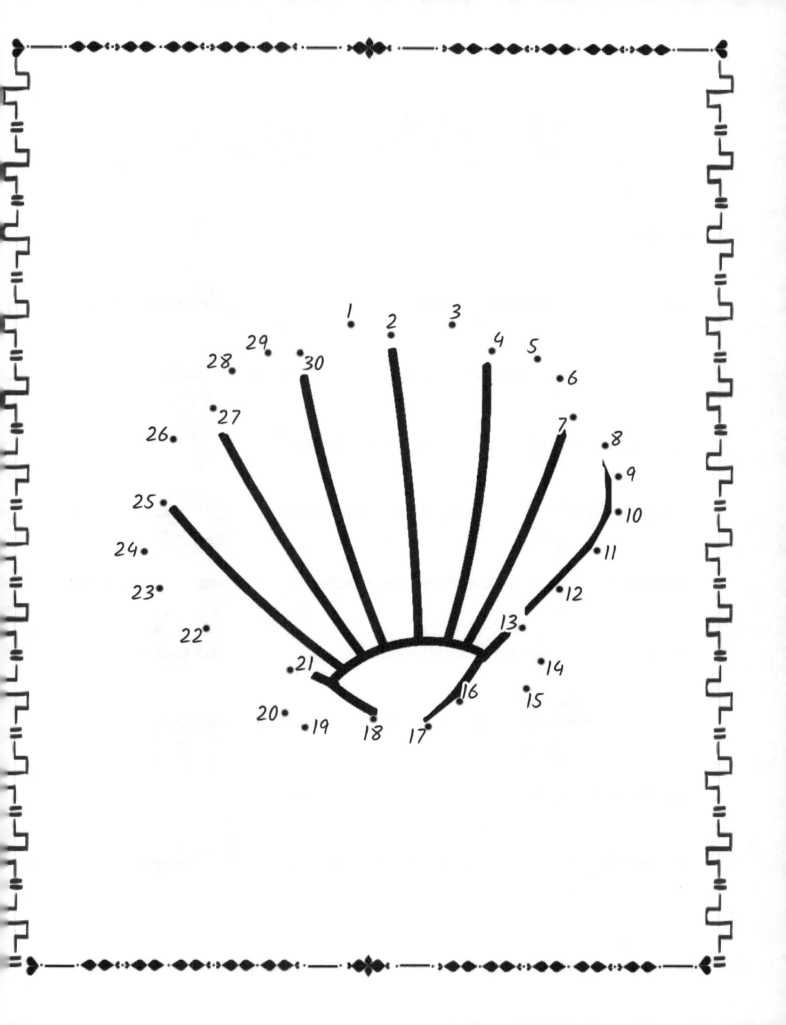

Shadow matching

Count and color

Maze game

Hawaii
CROSSWORD

Across:

4 A traditional Hawaiian dish made from taro root.

5 A musical instrument that is like a small guitar with four strings.

Down:

1 A type of shrub that has large colorful flowers.

2 A large fruit that has a thick shell with white flesh and liquid inside it and that grows on a palm tree.

3 A large marine reptile found in Hawaiian waters

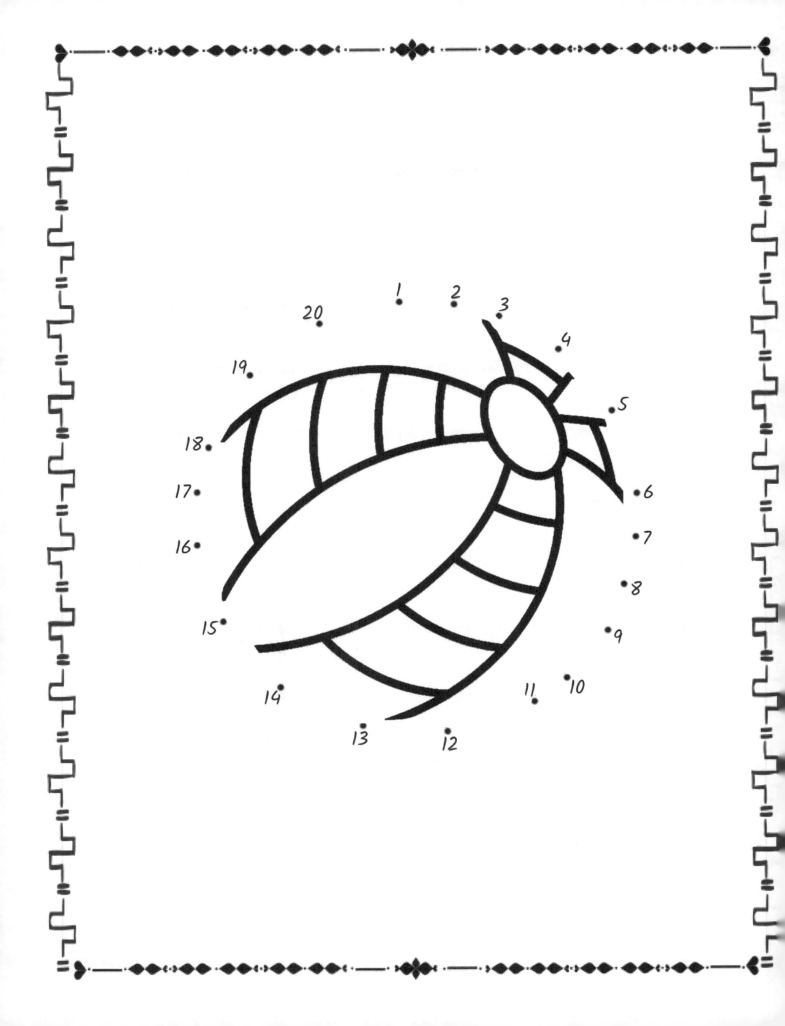

Count and color

Coloring Time

let's

Color

Blank page for no bleed through

Blank page for no bleed through

Blank page for no bleed through

Blank page for no bleed through

Blank page for no bleed through

Blank page for no bleed through

Blank page for no bleed through

Blank page for no bleed through

Blank page for no bleed through

Blank page for no bleed through

Blank page for no bleed through

Blank page for no bleed through

Blank page for no bleed through

Blank page for no bleed through

Blank page for no bleed through

Blank page for no bleed through

Blank page for no bleed through

Blank page for no bleed through

Blank page for no bleed through

Blank page for no bleed through

Solutions

KEY 01

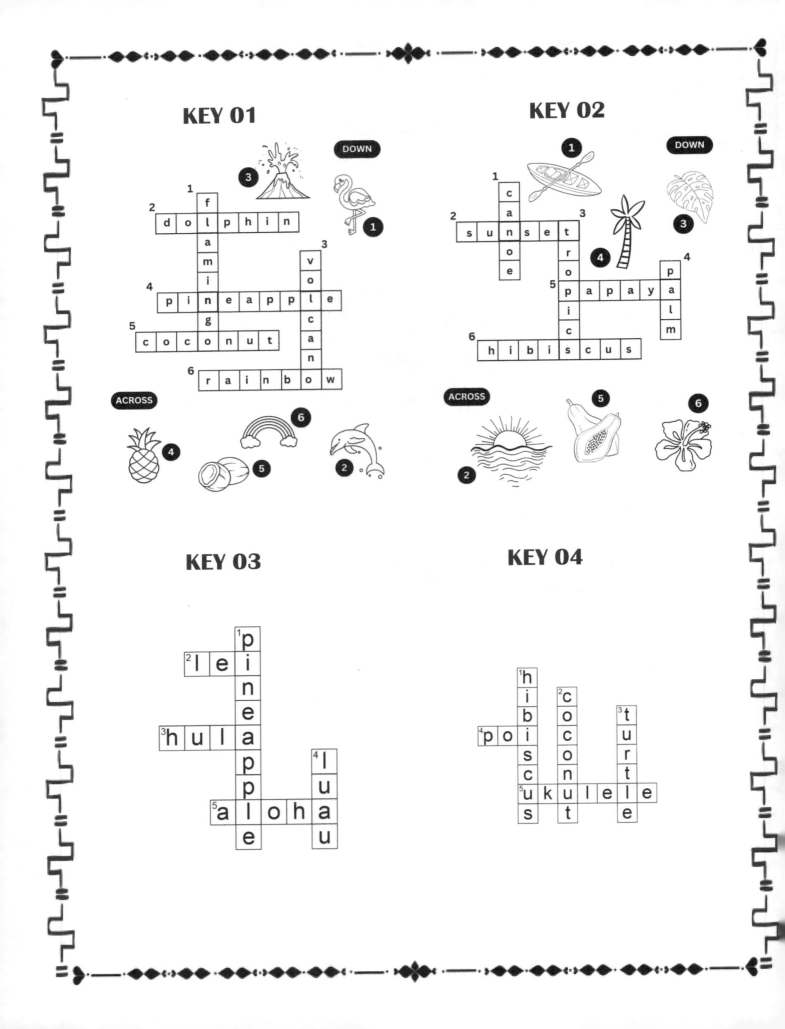

DOWN

1. flamingo
3. volcano

ACROSS

2. dolphin
4. pineapple
5. coconut
6. rainbow

KEY 02

DOWN

1. canoe
3. tropic
4. palm

ACROSS

2. sunset
5. papaya
6. hibiscus

KEY 03

2. le
3. hul
5. aloha
1. pineapple
4. luau

KEY 04

1. hibiscus
2. coconut
3. turtle
4. poi
5. ukulele

Count and color

4 **3** **4** **6** **2** **1**

Count and color

4 **3** **5** **6** **3** **2**

Count and color

⑤? ⑨? ⑦? ⑥?

Count and color

④? ⑤? ⑧? ⑦?

KEY 01

Maze game

KEY 02

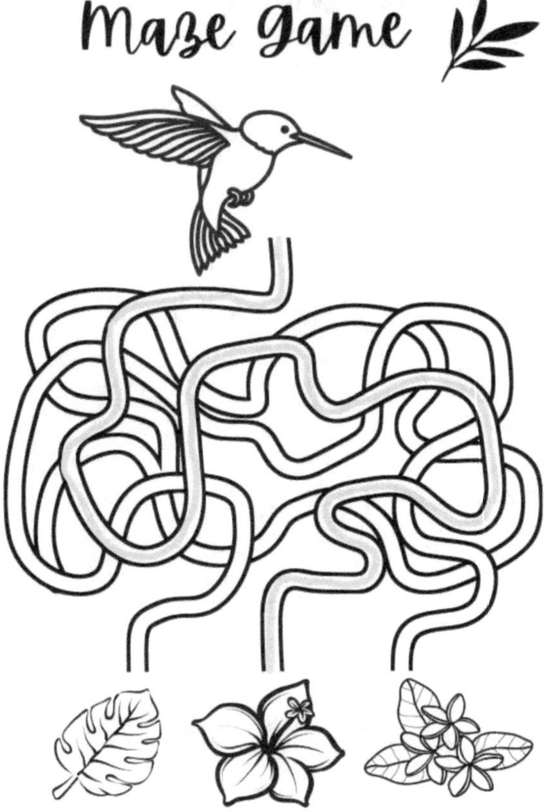

Maze game

KEY 03

Maze game

KEY 04

Maze game

KEY 05

Maze game

KEY 01

Spot 5 differences

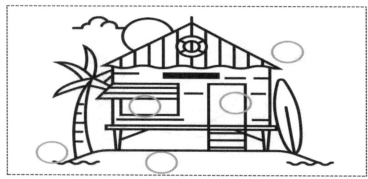

KEY 02

Spot 5 differences

Thank you for purchasing this Hawaii activity book for kids, we hope you and your family enjoy all the activities and facts inside.

Made in United States
Troutdale, OR
04/12/2025

30539981R00064